To

_____

From

_____

365 *Smiles a Year For Teachers*

365 Smiles a Year For Teachers

Copyright © 2005 by FaithPoint Press

Produced by Cliff Road Books

ISBN: 1-58173-492-1

Book design by Pat Covert

Printed in China

365 *Smiles a Year For Teachers*

FaithP✦int™
PRESS

An invincible determination can accomplish almost anything, and in this lies the great distinction between great men and little men.

Thomas Fuller

The difference between the right word and the almost right word is the difference between lightning and the lightning bug.

Mark Twain

A person can stand almost anything except a succession of ordinary days.

Johann Wolfgang von Goethe

Take the course opposite to custom, and you will almost always do well.

Jean Jacques Rousseau

A teacher who is attempting to teach without inspiring the pupil with a desire to learn is hammering on cold iron.

Horace Mann

A man can succeed at almost anything for which he has unlimited enthusiasm.

Charles M. Schwab

Performance stands out like a ton of diamonds. Non-performance can almost always be explained away.

Harold S. Geneen

I am always doing things I can't do; that's how I get to do them.

Pablo Picasso

The first idea that the child must acquire, in order to be actively disciplined, is that of the difference between good and evil; and the task of the educator lies in seeing that the child does not confound good with immobility and evil with activity.

Maria Montessori

Reason and judgement are the qualities of a leader.

Tacitus

Some men give up their designs when they have almost reached the goal; while others, on the contrary, obtain a victory by exerting, at the last moment, more vigorous efforts than ever before.

Herodotus

What is important is to keep learning, to enjoy challenge, and to tolerate ambiguity. In the end, there are no certain answers.

Martina Horner

Do you know the difference between education and experience? Education is when you read the fine print; experience is what you get when you don't.

Pete Seeger

Three keys to more abundant living: caring about others, daring for others, sharing with others.

William Arthur Ward

Some of the world's greatest feats were accomplished by people not smart enough to know they were impossible.

Doug Larson

January 16

Confidence ... thrives only on honesty, on honor, on the sacredness of obligation, on faithful performance. Without them, it cannot live.

Franklin D. Roosevelt

Too often we underestimate the power of a touch, a smile, a kind word, a listening ear, an honest compliment, or the smallest act of caring, all of which have the potential to turn a life around.

Leo Buscaglia

Every child is an artist. The problem is how to remain an artist once he grows up.

Pablo Picasso

Good teaching is
one-fourth preparation and
three-fourths theater.

Gail Godwin

Leaders aren't born; they are made. And they are made just like anything else, through hard work. And that's the price we'll have to pay to achieve that goal, or any goal.

Vincent Lombardi

Most of our obstacles would melt away if, instead of cowering before them, we should make up our minds to walk boldly through them.

Orison Swett Marden

If kids come to us from strong, healthy functioning families, it makes our job easier. If they do not come to us from strong, healthy, functioning families, it makes our job more important.

Barbara Colorose

Far and away the best prize that life offers is the chance to work hard at work worth doing.

Theodore Roosevelt

Appreciation is a wonderful thing.
It makes what is excellent in others
belong to us as well.

Voltaire

I would rather be able to appreciate things I cannot have than to have things I am not able to appreciate.

Elbert Hubbard

Courtesies of a small and trivial character are the ones which strike deepest in the gratefully and appreciating heart.

Henry Clay

Education is the movement
from darkness to light.
Allan Bloom

The young do not know enough to be prudent, and therefore they attempt the impossible, and achieve it, generation after generation.

Pearl Buck

Let us resolve to be masters, not the victims, of our history, controlling our own destiny without giving way to blind suspicions and emotions.

John F. Kennedy

There is more hunger for love and appreciation in this world than for bread.

Mother Teresa

Much learning does not teach understanding.

Heraclitus

He who has never learned to obey
cannot be a good commander.

Aristotle

Appreciation can make a day, even change a life. Your willingness to put it into words is all that is necessary.

Margaret Cousins

If there were no schools to take the children away from home part of the time, the insane asylums would be filled with mothers.

Edgar W. Howe

Accomplish something for yourself, not others.

Unknown

Modern cynics and skeptics ... see no harm in paying those to whom they entrust the minds of their children a smaller wage than is paid to those to whom they entrust the care of their plumbing.

John F. Kennedy

Neither books nor people have Velcro sides; there must be a bonding agent, someone who attaches child to book.

Jim Trelease

If you think you can do it, you can. If you believe you can do it, you will. If you trust you can do it, you will make a difference.

Catherine Ellis

When you've got something
to prove, there's nothing greater
than a challenge.

Terry Bradshaw

If a little dreaming is dangerous, the cure for it is not to dream less but to dream more, to dream all the time.

Marcel Proust

Double, no triple, our troubles, and we'd still be better off than any other people on earth. It is time that we recognized that ours was, in truth, a noble cause.

Ronald Reagan

I discovered I always have choices, and sometimes it's only a choice of attitude.

Judith M. Knowlton

We cannot hold a torch to
light another's path without
brightening our own.

Ben Sweetland

What happens to a man is less significant than what happens within him.

Louis L. Mann

Genius without education is like
silver in the mine.
Ben Franklin

Take the attitude of a student; never be too big to ask questions, never know too much to learn something new.

Og Mandino

We tend to live up to our expectations.

Earl Nightingale

The key to successful leadership today is influence, not authority.

Kenneth Blanchard

The wisest mind has
something yet to learn.
George Santayana

It's how you deal with failure that determines how you achieve success.

David Feherty

I never expect to lose. Even when I'm the underdog, I still prepare a victory speech.

H. Jackson Brown Jr.

Make your life a mission – not
an intermission.
Arnold Glasgow

Teachers are expected to reach unattainable goals with inadequate tools. The miracle is that at times they accomplish this impossible task.

Haim G. Ginott

Don't expect to build up the weak by pulling down the strong.

Calvin Coolidge

Leadership is the challenge to be something more than average.

Jim Rohn

Pretend that every single person you meet has a sign around his or her neck that says, "Make Me Feel Important." You will succeed in life.

Mary Kay Ash

Teaching is the profession that teaches all the other professions.

Unknown

Heroes became heroes flaws
and all. You don't have to be perfect
to fulfill your dream.

Peter McWilliams

For success, attitude is equally as important as ability.

Harry F. Banks

Learning. The kind of ignorance distinguishing the studious.

Ambrose Bierce

To educate a man in mind,
and not in morals, is to educate a
menace to society.

Theodore Roosevelt

There are no menial jobs, only menial attitudes.

William Bennett

An optimist may see a light where there is none, but why must the pessimist always run to blow it out?

Michel De Saint-Pierre

To be good is noble, but to teach others how to be good is nobler and less trouble.

Mark Twain

Leadership is the ability of a single individual through his or her actions to motivate others to higher levels of achievement.

Buck Rodgers

Live as you will have wished to have lived when you are dying.

Christian Furchtegott Gellert

A man is not finished
when he's defeated; he's finished
when he quits.

Richard M. Nixon

Learning without thought is labor lost; thought without learning is perilous.

Confucius

The fact we must remember is that we are educating students for a world that will not be ours but will be theirs. Give them a chance to be heard.

Carlos P. Romulo

Look well to this day. Yesterday is but a dream, and tomorrow is only a vision. But today well lived makes every yesterday a dream of happiness and every tomorrow a vision of hope. Look well therefore to this day.

Francis Gray

The problems of this world
cannot possibly be solved by
skeptics or cynics whose horizons
are limited by the obvious realities.
We need men who can dream of
things that never were.

John F. Kennedy

Nothing can stop the man with the right mental attitude from achieving his goal; nothing on earth can help the man with the wrong mental attitude.

W. W. Ziege

Teaching is the only major occupation of man for which we have not yet developed tools that make an average person capable of competence and performance. In teaching we rely on the "naturals," the ones who somehow know how to teach.

Peter Drucker

Don't bother just to be better than your contemporaries or predecessors. Try to be better than yourself.

William Faulkner

In teaching, you cannot see the fruit of a day's work. It is invisible and remains so, maybe for twenty years.

Jacques Barzun

Those who would make us
feel must feel themselves.

Charles Churchill

If I were asked to give what I consider the most useful bit of advice for all humanity, it would be this: Expect trouble as an inevitable part of life, and when it comes, hold your head high, look it squarely in the eye, and say, "I will be bigger than you. You cannot defeat me."

Ann Landers

I have found it advisable not to give too much heed to what people say when I am trying to accomplish something of consequence. Invariably, they proclaim it can't be done. I deem that the very best time to make the effort.

Calvin Coolidge

Education is simply the soul of a society as it passes from one generation to another.

G. K. Chesterton

There are only two ways to live your life. One is as though nothing is a miracle. The other is as if everything is.

Albert Einstein

A leader leads by example, whether he intends to or not.

Unknown

Learning is not attained by chance; it must be sought for with ardor and attended to with diligence.

Abigail Adams

Dream as if you'll live forever. Live as if you'll die today.

James Dean

Keep dreaming, for as long as you dream that dream might come true.

Unknown

We cannot change our past. We cannot change the fact that people act in a certain way. We cannot change the inevitable. The only thing we can do is play on the one string we have, and that is our attitude.

Charles Swindoll

My father gave me the greatest gift anyone could give another person. He believed in me.

Jim Valvano

I love living. I have some problems with my life, but living is the best thing they've come up with so far.

Neil Simon

The good teacher makes the poor student good and the good student superior. When our students fail, we, as teachers, too, have failed.

Marva Collins

Act as though it is impossible to fail.

Unknown

I am almost overwhelmed by the courage and dedication of teachers.

Sylvia Solomon

Efforts and courage are not enough without purpose and direction.

John F. Kennedy

The spirit, the will to win, and the will to excel are the things that endure. These qualities are so much more important than the events that occur.

Vincent Lombardi

The dream begins with a teacher who believes in you, who tugs and pushes and leads you to the next plateau, sometimes poking you with a sharp stick called "truth."

Dan Rather

The only way around is through.
Robert Frost

Do the hard jobs first. The easy jobs
will take care of themselves.

Dale Carnegie

A leader is a dealer in hope.

Napoleon Bonaparte

When you love people and have the desire to make a profound, positive impact upon the world, then will you have accomplished the meaning to live.

Sasha Azevedo

Education is the ability to listen to almost anything without losing your temper or your self-confidence.

Robert Frost

A dream is your creative vision for your life in the future. You must break out of your current comfort zone and become comfortable with the unfamiliar and the unknown.

Denis Waitley

The quality of a leader is reflected in the standards they set for themselves.

Ray Kroc

One never notices what has been done; one can only see what remains to be done.

Marie Curie

A big man is one who makes us feel bigger when we are with him.

John C. Maxwell

Education is a progressive discovery
of our own ignorance.

Will Durant

The rung of a ladder was never meant to rest upon, but only to hold a man's foot long enough to enable him to put the other somewhat higher.

Thomas Huxley

Treat people as if they were what they ought to be, and you help them to become what they are capable of being.

Johann Wolfgang von Goethe

It is hard to fail, but it is worse never to have tried to succeed. In this life we get nothing save by effort.

Theodore Roosevelt

The secret of teaching is to appear to have known all your life what you just learned this morning.

Unknown

It is the nature of man to rise to greatness if greatness is expected of him.

John Steinbeck

Slump, and the world slumps with you. Push, and you push alone.

Laurence J. Peter

The test of a good teacher is not how many questions he can ask his pupils that they will answer readily, but how many questions he inspires them to ask him which he finds it hard to answer.

Alice Wellington Rollins

Look over your shoulder now and then to be sure someone's following you.

Henry Gilmer

Get excited and enthusiastic about your own dream. This excitement is like a forest fire – you can smell it, taste it, and see it from a mile away.

Denis Waitley

People can be divided into two classes: those who go ahead and do something, and those people who sit still and inquire, why wasn't it done the other way?

Oliver Wendell Holmes

Leadership is based on a spiritual quality, the power to inspire the power to inspire others to follow.

Vincent Lombardi

The very spring and root of honesty
and virtue lie in good education.

Plutarch

Impossible is a word found only in a fool's dictionary.

Napoleon

To teach well, we need not say all
that we know, only what is useful
for the pupil to hear.

Unknown

Rule number one is, don't sweat the small stuff. Rule number two is, it's all small stuff.

Robert Eliot

When you have got an elephant by the hind leg, and he is trying to run away, it's best to let him run.

Abraham Lincoln

A wise man learns something new every day. The fool knows it already.

Unknown

We can easily manage if we will only take, each day, the burden appointed to it. But the load will be too heavy for us if we carry yesterday's burden over again today, and then add the burden of the morrow before we are required to bear it.

John Newton

Today is the tomorrow we
worried about yesterday.

Unknown

The toughest thing about success is that you've got to keep on being a success.

Irving Berlin

The man who removes a
mountain begins by carrying
away small stones.
Chinese Proverb

A leader takes people where they want to go. A great leader takes people where they don't necessarily want to go, but ought to be.

Rosalynn Carter

The mind is not a vessel to be filled,
but a fire to be ignited.

Plutarch

Reflect upon your present blessings, of which every man has plenty; not on your past misfortunes, of which all men have some.

Charles Dickens

Work for the fun of it, and the money will arrive some day.

Ronnie Milsap

Great leaders ... motivate large groups of individuals to improve the human condition.

John Kotter

Get action. Seize the moment.
Man was never intended to
become an oyster.

Theodore Roosevelt

One mark of a great educator
is the ability to lead students
out to new places where even the
educator has never been.

Thomas Groome

We must want for others,
not ourselves alone.
Eleanor Roosevelt

To lead people, walk beside them.

Lao-tzu

When you cannot make up your mind which of two evenly balanced courses of action you should take — choose the bolder.

William Joseph Slim

To teach is to learn twice.

Joseph Joubert

My idea of education is to unsettle the minds of the young and inflame their intellects.

Robert Maynard Hutchins

It is only the ignorant who despise education.

Publilius Syrus

I wash my hands of those
who imagine chattering to be
knowledge, silence to be ignorance,
and affection to be art.

Kahlil Gibran

Let us not become weary in doing good, for at the proper time we will reap a harvest if we do not give up.

Galatians 6:9

All grown-ups were once children,
though few of them remember it.

Antoine de Saint Exupéry

It is not the answer that
enlightens, but the question.

Eugene Ionesco Decouvertes

Learning is a treasure that will follow its owner everywhere.

Chinese Proverb

Courage is resistance to fear, mastery of fear — not absence of fear. Except a creature be part coward, it is not a compliment to say it is brave.

Mark Twain

What the caterpillar calls
the end, the rest of the world
calls a butterfly.

Lao-tzu

You do not lead by hitting people over the head – that's assault, not leadership.

Dwight D. Eisenhower

We're fools whether we dance or not, so we might as well dance.

Japanese Proverb

It's lack of faith that makes people afraid of meeting challenges, and I believe in myself.

Muhammad Ali

Life without liberty is like
a body without spirit.

Kahlil Gibran

Many of life's failures are people who did not realize how close they were to success when they gave up.

Thomas Edison

You are only as strong as your purpose; therefore let us choose reasons to act that are big, bold, righteous, and eternal.

Barry Munro

Education's purpose is to replace an empty mind with an open one.

Malcolm Forbes

Real education must ultimately be limited to men who insist on knowing; the rest is mere sheep-herding.

Ezra Pound

There are three things to remember when teaching: know your stuff; know whom you are stuffing; and then stuff them elegantly.

Lola May

We choose our joys and sorrows
long before we experience them.

Kahlil Gibran

I am only one, but still I am one. I cannot do everything, but still I can do something. I will not refuse to do the something I can do.

Helen Keller

The greatest discovery of my generation is that a man can alter his life simply by altering his attitude of mind.

William James

Who dares to teach must
never cease to learn.

John Cotton Dana

Smile. It increases your face value.

Dolly Parton

Live life today. Yesterday is gone,
and tomorrow may never come.

Unknown

Challenges are what make life interesting; overcoming them is what makes life meaningful.

Joshua J. Marine

Always bear in mind that your own
resolution to succeed is more
important than any other one thing.

Abraham Lincoln

June 9

You cannot be a leader and ask other
people to follow you unless you
know how to follow, too.

Sam Rayburn

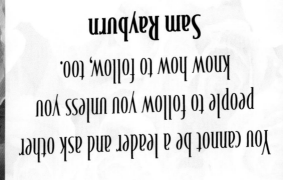

June 10

A pessimist sees only the dark side
of the clouds and mopes; a
philosopher sees both sides and
shrugs; an optimist doesn't see the
clouds at all because he's walking
on them.

Leonard Louis Levinson

The great aim of education is not
knowledge but action.

Herbert Spencer

A healthy attitude is contagious,
but don't wait to catch it from
others. Be a carrier.

Unknown

Always look at what you have left.
Never look at what you have lost.

Robert Schuller

Live daringly, boldly, fearlessly. Taste the relish to be found in competition – in having put forth the best within you.

Henry J. Kaiser

An optimist is a person who sees a green light everywhere, while a pessimist sees only the red stoplight. The truly wise person is colorblind.

Albert Schweitzer

It's not what happens to you, but
how you react to it that matters.

Epictetus

Tell me and I'll forget; show me and I may remember; involve me and I'll understand.

Chinese Proverb

Our happiness depends on the habit of mind we cultivate. So practice happy thinking every day. Cultivate the merry heart, develop the happiness habit, and life will become a continual feast.

Norman Vincent Peale

Attitudes are contagious. Is yours worth catching?

Unknown

I cannot teach anybody anything. I can only make them think.

Socrates

Leadership is action, not position.
Donald H. McGannon

Only those who dare to fail greatly
can ever achieve greatly.

Robert F. Kennedy

If I have seen farther than others, it is because I have stood on the shoulders of giants.

Sir Isaac Newton

The true teacher defends his pupils against his own personal influence. He inspires self-distrust. He guides their eyes from himself to the spirit that quickens him.

Amos Bronson Alcott

An education isn't how much you've committed to memory, or even how much you know. It's being able to differentiate between what you do know and what you don't.

Anatole France

Whether you think you can or
whether you think you can't,
you're right.

Henry Ford

If you aren't fired with enthusiasm,
you will be fired with enthusiasm.
Vincent Lombardi

To the uneducated, an A
is just three sticks.

A. A. Milne

Excellence is not a skill.
It is an attitude.

Ralph Marston

Be bold, be bold, and everywhere be bold.

Herbert Spencer

The best teachers teach from the heart, not from the book.

Unknown

Toughness is in the soul
and spirit, not in muscles.

Alex Karras

It's not the load that breaks you down; it's the way you carry it.

Lena Horne

Good timber does not grow with ease; the stronger the wind, the stronger the trees.

J. Willard Marriott

Unless life is lived for others,
it is not worthwhile.

Mother Teresa

The person who sends out positive thoughts activates the world around him positively and draws back to himself positive results.

Norman Vincent Peale

The mediocre teacher tells. The good teacher explains. The superior teacher demonstrates. The great teacher inspires.

William Arthur Ward

No executive has ever suffered
because his subordinates were
strong and effective.
Peter Drucker

When we do the best that we can, we never know what miracle is wrought in our life, or in the life of another.

Helen Keller

Children today are tyrants. They contradict their parents, gobble their food, and tyrannize their teachers.

Socrates

Sometimes you never see the fruits of your labors, but they are there, deep inside of the soul of the one you touched.

Dan Kelly

One of the tests of leadership is the ability to recognize a problem before it becomes an emergency.

Arnold Glasgow

It is the mark of an educated mind to be able to entertain a thought without accepting it.

Aristotle

Plunge boldly into the thick of life, and seize it where you will. It is always interesting.

Johann Wolfgang von Goethe

A leader, once convinced that a particular course of action is the right one, must be undaunted when the going gets tough.

Ronald Reagan

Attitude is a little thing that makes a big difference.

Winston Churchill

If you don't think every day is a good day, just try missing one.

Cavett Robert

We should be too big to take offense
and too noble to give it.

Abraham Lincoln

July 20

Life is ten percent what happens
to you, and ninety percent how
you respond to it.

Lou Holtz

The teacher who is indeed wise does not bid you to enter the house of his wisdom but rather leads you to the threshold of your mind.

Kahlil Gibran

"For I know the plans I have for you," declares the L ORD, "plans to prosper you and not to harm you, plans to give you hope and a future."

Jeremiah 29:11

It is better to light one small candle
than to curse the darkness.

Confucius

Things turn out best for the people who make the best of the way things turn out.

John Wooden

It'll be a great day when education gets all the money it wants, and the Air Force has to hold a bake sale to buy bombers.

Unknown

Realize that there are not hopeless situations; there are only people who take hopeless attitudes.

Norman Vincent Peale

There are no great people in this world, only great challenges that ordinary people rise to meet.

William Frederick Halsey Jr.

In seeking wisdom, the first step
is silence, the second listening,
the third remembering, the
fourth practicing, the
fifth – teaching others.

Ibn Gabirol

A smile is the light in your window that tells others that there is a caring, sharing person inside.

Denis Waitley

Only the educated are free.

Epictetus

Creativity is the power to connect
the seemingly unconnected.

William Plomer

Leadership is a combination of strategy and character. If you must be without one, be without the strategy.

Gen. H. Norman Schwarzkopf

To bring up a child in the way he should go, travel that way yourself once in a while.

Henry Wheeler Shaw

Never do things others can do and will do if there are things others cannot do or will not do.

Amelia Earhart

Go forward confidently,
energetically attacking problems,
expecting favorable outcomes.

Norman Vincent Peale

Never leave that 'til tomorrow
which you can do today.

Benjamin Franklin

Don't be afraid your life will end;
be afraid that it will never begin.

Grace Hansen

Difficulties are meant to rouse, not discourage. The human spirit is to grow strong by conflict.

William Ellery Channing

Lord, grant that I may always desire more than I accomplish.

Michelangelo

The foundation of every state is the education of its youth.

Diogenes Laertius

August 10

The ultimate measure of a person is not where they stand in moments of comfort and convenience, but where they stand in times of challenge and controversy.

Martin Luther King Jr.

One looks back with appreciation to the brilliant teachers, but with gratitude to those who touched our human feelings. The curriculum is so much necessary raw material, but warmth is the vital element for the growing plant and for the soul of the child.

Carl Jung

Teachers open the door, but you must enter by yourself.

Chinese Proverb

Only those who do nothing
make no mistakes.

Unknown

People who never achieve happiness are the ones who complain whenever they're awake, and whenever they're asleep, they are thinking about what to complain about tomorrow.

Adam Zimbler

A good leader takes a little more than his share of the blame, a little less than his share of the credit.

Arnold Glasgow

Sharing is healing.
Cathy Stone

The real voyage of discovery consists not in seeking new landscapes but in having new eyes.

Marcel Proust

The whole purpose of education is to turn mirrors into windows.

Sydney J. Harris

Wise teachers create an environment that encourages students to teach themselves.

Leonard Roy Frank

People rarely succeed unless they have fun in what they are doing.

Dale Carnegie

Upon our children – how they are taught – rests the fate, or fortune, of tomorrow's world.

B. C. Forbes

Give the pupils something to do, not something to learn; and the doing is of such a nature as to demand thinking; learning naturally results.

John Dewey

The enemy of the truth is very often not the lie – deliberate, contrived, and dishonest – but the myth – persistent, persuasive, and unrealistic.

John F. Kennedy

Education is what survives
when what has been learned
has been forgotten.

B. F. Skinner

He has the right to criticize
who has the heart to help.

Abraham Lincoln

Love truth, and pardon error.

Voltaire

It's really a wonder that I haven't dropped all my ideals, because they seem so absurd and impossible to carry out. Yet I keep them, because in spite of everything, I still believe that people are really good at heart.

Anne Frank

If you don't like something, change it. If you can't change it, change your attitude. Don't complain.

Maya Angelou

Although the world is very full of suffering, it is also full of the overcoming of it.

Helen Keller

When we share – that is poetry
in the prose of life.
Sigmund Freud

May he give you the desire of your heart and make all your plans succeed.

Psalm 20:4

Leadership is practiced not so much in words as in attitude and in actions.

Harold S. Geneen

Teachers who inspire know that teaching is like cultivating a garden, and those who would have nothing to do with thorns must never attempt to gather flowers.

Unknown

Life is an adventure in forgiveness.
Norman Cousins

Handle them carefully, for words
have more power than atom bombs.

Pearl Strachan Hurd

Not in rewards, but in the strength
to strive, the blessing lies.

J. T. Towbridge

Better than a thousand days
of diligent study is one day
with a great teacher.

Japanese Proverb

Our prayers should be for blessings in general, for God knows best what is good for us.

Socrates

Teachers who inspire realize there will always be rocks in the road ahead of us. They will be stumbling blocks or stepping stones; it all depends on how we use them.

Unknown

Education is the best
provision for old age.
Aristotle

The hardest arithmetic to master is that which enables us to count our blessings.

Eric Hoffer

Act as if what you do makes a difference. It does.

William James

Weakness of attitude becomes
weakness of character.

Albert Einstein

Man was designed for accomplishment, engineered for success, and endowed with the seeds of greatness.

Zig Ziglar

Keep your fears to yourself,
but share your courage
with others.

Robert Louis Stevenson

Leadership should be more participative than directive, more enabling than performing.

Mary D. Poole

Until all of us have made it,
none of us have made it.

Rosemary Brown

Blessed are those who can give without remembering and take without forgetting.

Elizabeth Bibesco

It is literally true that you can succeed best and quickest by helping others to succeed.

Napoleon Hill

Don't be content with being average. Average is as close to the bottom as it is to the top.

Unknown

Tenderness and kindness are not signs of weakness and despair but manifestations of strength and resolution.

Kahlil Gibran

I am not bound to win, but I am bound to be true. I am not bound to succeed, but I am bound to live up to what light I have.

Abraham Lincoln

You don't realize how strong a person really is until you see them at their weakest moment.

Unknown

September 23

Teaching is leaving a vestige of one self in the development of another. And surely the student is a bank where you can deposit your most precious treasures.

Eugene P. Bertin

September 24

You can preach a better
sermon with your life than
with your lips.
Oliver Goldsmith

Leaders must be close enough to relate to others, but far enough ahead to motivate them.

John Maxwell

The art of teaching is the
art of assisting discovery.
Mark Van Doren

My attitude is never to be satisfied,
never enough, never.

Bela Karolyi

A leader is one who knows the way,
goes the way, and shows the way.

John C. Maxwell

It is possible to store the mind with a million facts and still be entirely uneducated.

Alec Bourne

Surely the world we live in is but the world that lives in us.

Daisy Bates

You can't lead anyone else farther than you have gone yourself.

Gene Mauch

Educate your children to self-control, to the habit of holding passion and prejudice and evil tendencies subject to an upright and reasoning will, and you have done much to abolish misery from their future lives and crimes from society.

Daniel Webster

How far that little candle
throws his beams! So shines a
good deed in a weary world.

William Shakespeare

Life's problems wouldn't be called "hurdles" if there wasn't a way to get over them.

Unknown

Do not wait for leaders.
Do it alone, person to person.

Mother Teresa

A student is not above his teacher,
but everyone who is fully trained
will be like his teacher.

Luke 6:40

The fool doth think he is wise, but the wise man knows himself to be a fool.

William Shakespeare

What sculpture is to a
block of marble, education is
to a human soul.

Joseph Addison

A teacher's purpose is not to create students in his own image, but to develop students who can create their own image.

Unknown

If you judge people, you have no time to love them.

Mother Teresa

Our attitude toward life determines
life's attitude toward us.

Earl Nightingale

To accomplish great things
we must first dream, then visualize,
then plan ... believe ... act!

Alfred A. Montapert

Hitch your wagon to a star.

Ralph Waldo Emerson

Teaching should be full of ideas
instead of stuffed with facts.

Unknown

It is not because things are difficult
that we do not dare; it is because we
do not dare that they are difficult.

Seneca

It is the supreme art of the teacher to awaken joy in creative expression and knowledge.

Albert Einstein

If you put a small value on yourself, rest assured that the world will not raise your price.

Unknown

Leaders are problem
solvers by talent and temperament,
and by choice.

Harlan Cleveland

There is nothing that cannot be achieved by firm imagination.

Japanese Proverb

The whole art of teaching is only the art of awakening the natural curiosity of young minds for the purpose of satisfying it afterwards.

Anatole France

It doesn't matter how many say it cannot be done or how many people have tried it before; it's important to realize that whatever you're doing, it's your first attempt at it.

Wally Amos

Yesterday ended last night. Every day is a new beginning. Learn the skill of forgetting. And move on.

Norman Vincent Peale

There is little difference in people, but that little difference makes a big difference. That little difference is attitude. The big difference is whether it is positive or negative.

W. Clement Stone

There are no rules here. We're trying to accomplish something.

Thomas Edison

Positive thinking is the key to success in business, education, pro football, anything that you can mention. I go out there thinking that I'm going to complete every pass.

Ron Jaworski

The first task of a leader
is to keep hope alive.

Joe Batten

Work joyfully and peacefully,
knowing that right thoughts and
right efforts will inevitably bring
about right results.

James Allen

A man's mind, stretched by a new idea, can never go back to its original dimension.

Oliver Wendell Holmes

The best teacher is the one who suggests rather than dogmatizes and inspires his listener with the wish to teach himself.

Edward Bulwer-Lytton

A child can ask questions that a
wise man cannot answer.

Unknown

I want to be thoroughly used up
when I die, for the harder I work,
the more I live. I rejoice in life
for its own sake.

George Bernard Shaw

The best executive is one who has sense enough to pick good people to do what he wants done, and self-restrain enough to keep from meddling with them while they do it.

Theodore Roosevelt

Every noble work is
at first impossible.
Thomas Carlyle

The brain is like muscle. When we think well, we feel good. Understanding is a kind of ecstasy.

Carl Sagan

A pessimist is one who makes
difficulties of his opportunities, and
an optimist is one who makes
opportunities of his difficulties.

Harry S. Truman

The important thing is to not stop questioning.

Albert Einstein

Education is helping the child realize
his potentialities.

Erich Fromm

Too often we give children answers to remember instead of problems to solve.

Roger Lewin

If you view all the things that happen to you, both good and bad, as opportunities, then you operate out of a higher level of consciousness.

Les Brown

Whatever you vividly imagine,
ardently desire, sincerely believe,
and enthusiastically act upon ...
must inevitably come to pass.

Paul J. Meyer

What the teacher is, is more important than what he teaches.

Karl Menninger

Believe it is possible to solve your problem. Tremendous things happen to the believer. So believe the answer will come. It will.

Norman Vincent Peale

A good teacher is like a candle – it consumes itself to light the way for others.

Unknown

At the center of your being, you have the answer. You know who you are, and you know what you want.

Lao-tzu

The secret of a leader lies in the tests he has faced over the whole course of his life and the habit of action he develops in meeting those tests.

Gail Sheehy

It is not fair to ask of others what you are unwilling to do yourself.

Eleanor Roosevelt

Pull the string, and it will follow wherever you wish. Push it, and it will go nowhere at all.

Dwight D. Eisenhower

Attitudes are more important
than facts.

Carl Menninger

To change and to change for the better are two different things.

German Proverb

The time is always right to do what is right.

Martin Luther King Jr.

The function of leadership is to produce more leaders, not more followers.

Ralph Nader

The larger the island of knowledge,
the longer the shoreline of wonder.

Ralph W. Sockman

A teacher affects eternity;
he can never tell where
his influence stops.

Henry Adams

What we want is to see the child in pursuit of knowledge, and not knowledge in pursuit of the child.

George Bernard Shaw

November 24

Never tell people how to do things.
Tell them what to do, and they will
surprise you with their ingenuity.

George Patton

I hear and I forget. I see
and remember. I do
and I understand.

Confucius

We expect teachers to handle
teenage pregnancy, substance abuse,
and the failings of the family.
Then we expect them to educate
our children.

John Sculley

Every good and perfect gift is from above, coming down from the Father of the heavenly lights, who does not change like shifting shadows.

James 1:17

Ability is what you're capable of doing. Motivation determines what you do. Attitude determines how well you do it.

Lou Holtz

Never be afraid to try something new. Remember, amateurs built the ark. Professionals built the Titanic.

Unknown

If you can dream it, you can do it.

Walt Disney

Reading is to the mind what exercise is to the body.

Sir Richard Steele

The great obstacle to discovering the shape of the earth, the continents, and the ocean was not ignorance but the illusion of knowledge.

Daniel J. Boorstin

Leaders who win the respect of others are the ones who deliver more than they promise, not the ones who promise more than they can deliver.

Mark Clement

Forget about all the reasons
why something may not work.
You only need to find one good
reason why it will.

Robert Anthony

We are all in the gutter, but some of us are looking at the stars.

Oscar Wilde

Nothing is good or bad,
but thinking makes it so.

William Shakespeare

What nobler employment, or more valuable to the state, than that of the man who instructs the rising generation?

Marcus Tullius Cicero

An army of sheep led by a
lion would defeat an army of
lions led by a sheep.

Arab Proverb

While we try to teach our children all about life, our children teach us what life is all about.

Angela Schwindt

When you love people and have
the desire to make a profound,
positive impact upon the world,
then will you have accomplished the
meaning to live.

Sasha Azevedo

The beautiful thing about learning is that no one can take it away from you.

B. B. King

You don't lead by pointing and telling people some place to go. You lead by going to that place and making a case.

Ken Kesey

It is not the answer that enlightens, but the question.

Eugene Ionesco Decouvertes

There is no joy in possession
without sharing.
Erasmo da Rotterdam

December 15

And we are put on earth a little space that we might learn to bear the beams of love.

William Blake

I am learning all the time. The tombstone will be my diploma.

Eartha Kitt

I don't think much of a man
who is not wiser today than
he was yesterday.

Abraham Lincoln

December 18

Nothing in the world can take the place of persistence. Talent will not; nothing is more common than unsuccessful men with talent. Genius will not; unrewarded genius is almost a proverb .... Persistence and determination are omnipotent.

Calvin Coolidge

December 19

Enter every activity without giving mental recognition to the possibility of defeat. Concentrate on your strengths instead of your weaknesses, on your powers instead of your problems.

Paul J. Meyer

A good teacher is a
master of simplification and an
enemy of simplism.

Louis A. Berman

Leadership is getting someone to do what they don't want to do, to achieve what they want to achieve.

Tom Landry

Men make history, and not the other way around. In periods where there is no leadership, society stands still. Progress occurs when courageous, skillful leaders seize the opportunity to change things for the better.

Harry S. Truman

A life spent making mistakes is not only more honorable but more useful than a life spent doing nothing.

George Bernard Shaw

A master can tell you what he expects of you. A teacher, though, awakens your own expectation.

Patricia Neal

December 25

I can do everything through him
who gives me strength.

Philippians 4:13

He who opens a school door
closes a prison.
Victor Hugo

Effective leadership is putting first things first. Effective management is discipline, carrying it out.

Stephen Covey

A word of encouragement during a failure is worth more than an hour of praise after success.

Unknown

There are two lasting bequests we can hope to give our children. One of these is roots, the other, wings.

Hodding Carter

A BMW can't take you as
far as a diploma.

Joyce Myers

When I am trusting
myself as fully as
everything in my
this by falling int
often mira

Shakti

There are two lasting bequests we can hope to give our children. One of these is roots, the other, wings.

Hodding Carter

A BMW can't take you as
far as a diploma.
Joyce Myers

When I am trusting and being myself as fully as possible, everything in my life reflects this by falling into place easily, often miraculously.

Shakti Gawain